CROSSING the RIVER

SELECTED POEMS
Translated from the Hebrew

Moshe Dor

Moshe Dor

CROSSING the RIVER

SELECTED POEMS

Translated from the Hebrew

Edited by Seymour Mayne

CANADIAN CATALOGUING IN PUBLICATION DATA

Dor, Moshe, 1932-
Crossing the river : selected poems of Moshe Dor

Translated from Hebrew.
ISBN 0-88962-418-6

I. Mayne, Seymour, 1944- . II. Title.

PJ5054.D6C76 1989 892.4'1 C89-09402-X

Published by MOSAIC PRESS, P.O. Box 1032, Oakville, Ontario, L6J 5E9, Canada. Offices and warehouse at 1252 Speers Road, Units 1 & 2, Oakville, Ontario, L6L 5N9, Canada.

Mosaic Press acknowledges the assistance of the Canada Council and the Ontario Arts Council in support of its publishing programme.

The author and editor wish to thank the Institute for the Translation of Hebrew Literature for its support and encouragement.

Design by Rita Vogel.
Typeset by Bambam Graphics & Design.
Cover illustration and design by Marion Black.
Printed and bound in Canada.

ISBN 0-88962-418-6 PAPER

MOSAIC PRESS:
In Canada:
MOSAIC PRESS, 1252 Speers Road, Units 1&2, Oakville, Ontario L6L 5N9, Canada. P.O. Box 1032, Oakville, Ontario L6J 5E9

In the United States:
Distributed to the trade in the United States by: Kampmann National Book Network, Inc., 4720-A Boston Way, Lanham, MD, 20706, USA

In the U.K.:
John Calder (Publishers) Ltd., 18 Brewer Street, London, W1R 4A5, England

The poems included in this collection were translated from the Hebrew by Keith Bosley, Ann Darr, Ruth Fainlight, Anat Feinberg, Elaine Feinstein, Richard Flantz, Bernhard Frank, Barbara Goldberg, Denis Johnson, Francis Landy, Jean Nordhaus, Chaim Pessah, Anthony Rudolf, Edna Sharoni, Alan Sillitoe, Myra Sklarew, Henry Taylor, Mark Whiteis-Helm, and the editor.

CONTENTS

PREFACE

Moshe Dor writes evocatively about his childhood years growing up in Tel Aviv. Spreading out from the coast, the city and the surrounding landscape offered a rich variety of colours, faces and experiences to the growing consciousness that would come to maturity in the later work of a poet.

> In the early thirties Tel Aviv was a little white town and the gleaming sands of gold fell in bewitching folds towards the sea, which was a vast haven between blue and green. The coarse *zifzif* sand rustled under one's bare toes. Camel caravans passed, bells clanging on their swaying necks. The Moslem cemetery was a mystery where fearful possibilities lurked among the tombstones. Wild vines clothed the hills....
>
> Two magnificent sycamores grew in our yard. By day birds held a permanent celebration in their branches. By night bats glided to and from the tops...The sycamores spread a tremendous green canopy over the sand, their roots twisting endlessly, their fruit falling all around, sticky, wormy and bird-pecked.

Along with the work of other poets of his generation, much of his earlier writing draws inspiration from the land and landscape of Israel. In his poetry the tension between past and present, between city and hinterland, between fruition and decay heightens the poet's search and anguish. However these opposites find form and expression, there is a sense of possibility–if not immediately in the public world, then at least in the imagination. Whatever he sees has a deeper significance; he reads the world and he offers his poems as commentary. The Hebrew text contains within itself the personal and historical archaeology that must be deciphered, and it finds its own pattern of order generated by contemplation and insight.

Moshe Dor's commanding body of work began to draw notice outside of Israel in the 1970s with the publication of an introductory selection of his poems in translation. Since then many more translators have been challenged to render his unmistakable voice into English. What is remarkable to note are the cycles of renewal that typify each period of his writing. The epigrammatic and politically directed poems of the 1970s and early 1980s–written in response to the wars and turbulence in the Middle East–give way to sequences of intense love poems.

In a bold way the poet returns to the search but now it is tempered by the experience and perspective of age and by a greater sense of vulnerability to time. The landscape in the foreground now takes the figure of the feminine, which in turn acts as a redemptive counterpart to the suffering and imponderables of the political arena.

Dor is a lyrical poet par excellence. His poems link together so that the sudden and intense moments create a pattern of insights and a poetic world. His eclectic poetics allows him to draw on a variety of sources–not least of which are Jewish Scriptures and liturgy–including Russian symbolism, Anglo-American modernism, and twentieth century poetry from the language basin of the Mediterranean. Yet it is all transmuted through his very Hebrew accents and imagination which translate themselves readily beyond his particular language and personal world.

> The little houses have disappeared. The bells on the camels' long necks are silent. The horizon is hidden behind tall buildings. The sycamores have been cut down...My Tel Aviv is hiding. God's countenance does not smile down on me from a sky that is lower than it used to be.
>
> She hides, and I seek her, in love and despair. Through jammed streets poisoned with gasoline fumes I stalk the scent of jasmine that has fled down bluish tunnels: I know I can never reach it. But from the sycamores a storm of birds bursts out, boldly, gloriously, towards the sun.

In Moshe Dor's poems the words in their passage suggest shapes and forms always moving in the direction of poetic insight.

S. M.

I

1954-1969

HONEYCOMB

The green bible
of my ancestors
opens
to page after page

In groundsel, wild garlic, bloodstone
they mutter in a whisper

A breeze of myrrh on my forehead eyelids lips
blows through the stations of this new nation
In dark roots I search
for the honeycomb of Jonathan

When I find it
the scales will fall from the eyes
of the lonely ones
who will barter their firstborn rights
and their living breath
for the sweetness of the holy begetting

In groundsel, wild garlic, bloodstone
my ancestors
sow the pages of the green bible
and in the wind of myrrh

they flutter towards the open spaces
until dusk

Translated by Seymour Mayne

SWEET PORRIDGE

My son opens the gates of the world
as he eats his sweet porridge.
God smiles in his blue eyes at the world.
I stand by him like the dead giants of ages past
and long for the sweetness of his porridge
but the terrible angel raises his hand to kill me.
Day and night we wrestle,
then my son licks his little sweet porridge-smeared
fingers
murmuring the two syllables of light
"Dad dy"
and I break the terrible angel's neck
before he can touch the hollow of my thigh.
Then the gates of the world open like my son's
eyes
with the blue of space through them
and reaching to God.

Translated by Chaim Pessah

AT A LOSS

I am at a loss on this very street
whose houses and gardens are arranged coffee-table neat
yet my hand is in my son's hand and his glance is anchored
   in my face.
That his boat may not budge I pretend to bravery and manners.
Even as the demon's wing beats at my back
and the warm air glides in waves across my trembling cheeks
I go on smiling (my Lord, naked I stand before You
and vast is the night all about)
and bend over my son:
"Look, a bird! Look, a cat!"
I am at a loss on this very street.

Translated by Bernhard Frank

HAMSIN*

A shuddering travels down her thighs.
Her nipples harden into stone.
A veil of glass shields her eyes
and she cannot tell if an angel's hand
lifts the hem of her dress, or slowly
and with a terrible pleasure, the devil's
hoof caresses the slopes of her belly.

Somebody seals her eyelids with white fire.

Translated by Barbara Goldberg

**Heatwave*

A POEM FOR THE DAY OF ATONEMENT

Your hair smells like nothing I know.
Water flows between us and you
are not covered. I taste you
by increments, as the hours
pass through us, bittersweet.
Some say we must return to duties,
to obligations. Others speak
of passion. A dense darkness
blows through your hair. I own
only half of what I must possess.
Don't be the death of me. My sins
shall not be atoned. You emerge
unscathed. Your flesh is always
ravenous. When I am consumed,
you are nourished.

Translated by Barbara Goldberg

PAPER BOAT

Our thighs do not touch.
A green sea sways between us
in a small park in an anonymous tow
bare of heroic statues and fountains
where the hushed sunlight holds
conversations with faded oaks
and dusty cypresses. Your face wears
its faraway look and then you sink back
against the bench, a migratory bird
weary of flight. But our thighs
do not touch. And on the green sea
bobbing between us, Death
dressed in an absurd sailor's suit
sails a boat of candy wrappers.

Translated by Barbara Goldberg

INVITE ME TO SUPPORT YOUR ARM

Invite me to support your arm. I
must hold on to you. In 1932
it was a different fashion.
When I screamed for the first time
someone heard. The body was earth
not only because it was written that way.
        Now people
are not afraid of lips that scream
in the forbidden sand. If they subtract me
from the total sum, the result will be
        a round cipher.
Invite me to support your arm. I am entitled
to expect that from you before forgetfulness
sweeps over both of us. The moon makes
the sea froth. My deep-rooted fear and
        your compassion–
upon all your works.

Translated by Seymour Mayne

AT FIRST

At first you wait
from moment to moment
Afterwards, from day to day
From month to month
From year to year
And then
from death to death

Translated by Seymour Mayne

XANADU REVISITED

"In Xanadu did Kublah Khan..."
S.T. Coleridge

We arrived in Xanadu as planned and on time.
Our camels were loaded up and our money bags filled.
The walls were in ruins, the palaces gutted by fire.
The rose gardens had been trampled. The piles of bodies
were already stinking.
The Great Khan had been stabbed on the threshold
of his harem. His face was
distorted in death. We recognized him by his dress
and his crescent-shaped ornaments.
The sky was as blue as the water of the artificial pond
used to be. Now it stood stagnant and foul.
We didn't even allow our camels to kneel down. We
turned back.
Something lay shattered at the bottom of our memory
like a black vase of glass.
As we departed through the gates the sun burned on our
heads.
For a long time we were silent. Later the tales
were born.

Translated by Seymour Mayne

TIME IS MEASURED

Time is measured between steps.
In a hallway's measurements, hand
stretching to flick the light-switch,
the figure blooming from darkness, then
the concealment of the face.
"You don't look like yesterday or the day before."
What's yesterday? What the day before? What
security derives from headlines, from the smiles
of politicians and from their solemn looks,
from the study of old passages?
The poet stumbles from poem to poem

and from rage to rage. Today
armoured cars drove off to anywhere
leaving the smell of fuel and a blue smoke.
The hallway closed back to its darkness
and 3000 years later the hand flicked
the light-switch.
"Sweetheart," cracked lips
were murmuring in the night
while the sterile thunders
of guns opened up in the sky.

Translated by Denis Johnson

DOES DAVID STILL PLAY BEFORE YOU

Does David still play before you
on the golden harp?
And Solomon,
does he still invent, in your hearing,
his fox fables?

And from which field does Elijah take off
in a chariot of fire and with horses of fire?
and Ezekiel,
what being hammers him, with what creature
does he struggle in the stormy, shining substance?

And among curls of incense,
does still to forgive and love
plead the face, paler than a cloud,
of Jesus, with the Yellow Star?

And from out which savage Bible
of erupting, extinguished suns
do your hands, hardened
in the arteries, grope regretfully to tear
up disappointed promises?

Translated by Denis Johnson

HABIT

More than anything else I'm afraid of habit.
The frontier tears not only the earth apart
        but also people
who grow used to the rift. At the end you get used
        to hatred
as a part of your life. The party of the desperate
is being turned into a gathering of cutlery, empty
        faces, eyes
that have grown weary of looking straight ahead.
        For some time now
love is not the moving force. In the meantime
everything is going along as it did before. Deals
        without the passion
for decision. Postponements that have already become
        delays for their own sakes. Hollow names.
Finally even your own two hands
that were meant to perform the actions
are alien to you.
Now you have to cut across yourself in order to reach
        yourself.
You won't even start. It's too far.
A frontier, after all, is no game.

Translated by Seymour Mayne

PINE CONE

This brown, fragile cone lies in your palm:
don't clench it unless you want it shattered.
A fist suits those who divide and rule;
loosen, loosen your fingers:
a breeze steals through the breaches,
silently slipping in,
and the cone's scales snuggle
        up to your naked skin.

Stranger, what else do you desire?

Translated by Seymour Mayne

GOING BACK

According to the landmarks
I had come back to my starting line:
a gas station, a wounded olive trunk,
a ruined stone house.

Only your face
is not recognizable,
I shut it in my palms, deeply gazing.
Did we meet sometime? Sleep together?
Did I speak to you horrible,

loving words?
A gas station, wounded olive trunk, ruined stone house
do not strive to be more than they are,
but your face, breathing between my palms,

breaks some dark continuum
of which the naming
would be the naming also of myself, my true mission.
I can sleep beside you here,
from gas station to olive trunk to stone house
and when I awake, the seventy years
we are condemned to will be finished
and I no wiser than I was and
you no more open than you were
and all the deep slumbering
in the world will not have smoothed
even one wrinkle in my life, even one
storm between your breasts.

Translated by Denis Johnson

WOUNDS

"Una cancion es una herida de amor
que nos abrieron las cosas."
Gabriela Mistral

The wounds of love
are healed.
The words
will be dulled.
The voice
will not make itself heard.

The wounds of metal
are real.
The withering
flower of someone's manhood
is flung across the wide starlessness.
The torn chest clutches
the flare-bomb, the words
retreating, stumbling, their eyes scarred.

The wounds of love have knit.
The wounds
of metal are fresh, the blood is like dew,
golden nightingales will grow calm
emerging from the storm in the arteries,
fluttering over the white virginity of bone.
The words will move into twilight.

Translated by Denis Johnson

NOTES FOR AN ARMENIAN BIOGRAPHY

The zodiac does not encircle
the head of Astrik Bartevian, Armenian,
tailor, thin, large-eyed, sewing
his life into stitches here in

his home, an alley wholly
stone: not a river, no poplars
on its banks, and the old language
patch on patch. His chest sinks

as if he leans permanently to meditate
on hopelessness. He does not want payment
when the needle flies over the trousers.
The king does not pitch his tent

by the river, there even the eyes
of the crucified one become stones.
Sometimes, talking to the whore from
down the alley, listening more than speaking,

he flares slightly his nostrils
into the sweet dark perfume. A
very lonely man, who once dreamed
he weaved gold brocade for the archbishop's robe,

forgetting the elemental dictum of blackness,
who once in his dreaming sailed the boat
of the moon home, where he had never been,
where he wept between white peaks while

the grass flared like a green madness
on those slopes. Astrik
Bartevian, Armenian, when the thunderhead
of bells tears open around him, gives

thanks that his fate is ordained,
that he lives in a holy city and sews
with decaying fingers shrouds
for little stone birds.

Translated by Denis Johnson

II

1970-1979

MORNING

Here is another clear morning descending
to pluck figs in the sun's orchards,
another golden furrow opened
in Father's high forehead.
Gather flocks
to the pastures in the sky
and we shall feel the shade, green, fertile,
as little bells jingle in our eyes.

And from the edges of the Bible,
silently, birds drop to pick
red berries from the breast of the young shepherd
whose reflection is a seal on the heart of the stream.

Translated by Denis Johnson

A DEMENTED TREE

A demented tree
growing in a crumbling house.
The top branches
have already burst the roof, toward
conjectured skies, possible to define
no more than the tree is possible to name.
A demented tree whose
roots already gnaw the floor,
sucking up memories, the lost
lust, dusty heartbreaks.
A totally demented tree:
in fact the crumbling is perhaps
a desire of the bark, a fermentation
of the sap, a quivering
that will not release my fingers
when the skin craves the security
of your nakedness like a stripped house
longing for its wallpaper,
for the secrecy of curtains,
for a door shut against
the greenish, savage goring by stars.

Translated by Denis Johnson

SHALLOW

1.

The shallow waters are already thinly
layered with ice. Surrounding them, the oaks
stand in their helpless effoliation.
And an anonymous dark bird
circles endlessly, crying
in an odd, incomprehensible bird's voice,
nailing
up shreds of sky and pulling them down again.

2.

Now to nail like a shred of sky
the grey forehead, sick with permanent doubt,
to a mossy oak trunk, now
to sink in this leafy abyss, rustling with death,
to sink deeper, so that
the colour, the sound, the depth
are totally forgotten, only the bitter voice
remaining, a dark bird finished
trying to interpret its own cry,
circling over and over, circling
purposelessly, endlessly, as the ice closes in.

Translated by Denis Johnson

YOU ARE RIGHT, YOU KNOW

You are right, you know. It definitely depends
on your point of view. From here
you see a date tree, a red-tiled house, an arabesque
and no block of flats, as if a memory-
reserve. And today is December 1, and outside it is
summery weather. There will be
war perhaps, no, there will not. You
said: Sometimes it is enough to have a plot
of sky, nothing more, and just there the angel Gabriel
will blow his horn. I don't know names
of angels. Ripples of memories in a transparent time
and summery weather on December 1. Incredible.
A date tree, a red-tiled house, an
arabesque and no block of flats. And war, perhaps
yes, perhaps no. The voice of the turtle-dove like
the voice of the horn. You
said. Only a piece of sky and full
of angels' wings. You are
right. It depends on your point of view.

Translated by Ruth Fainlight

THE DWELLING

on alien ground I dwelt and also
I ate on the Day of Atonement unatoned
not even heretic my
eyes are rubies my mouth beaten gold
purple the thread in my beard

I am lord over 127 provinces
and frost in my bones spreads and pitch
plasters my palms

when I determined to build an ark
in order myself to escape on
alien ground a dark bird
cried his dark voice

I did not learn his name as I sank to the depths
my eyes they are rubies my mouth beaten gold
and purple the thread in my beard
a day of atoning for sin
I have not even yet fearlessly
set forward my heresy there is no faith
in my bones I am lord
127 provinces

I wept remembering Zion in the cold
when kingdoms
fall and dark are the wings of the bird
its cries a sea
of darkness I do not know my name

Translated by Denis Johnson

THE WORLD SHRINKS

The world shrinks against me. Morning
and evening close the limits of desire. A breeze
stops at the shoreline.

Why, world, do you shrink
like a withered orange?

Child, under
the tarmac lies a plot of earth
with oleanders and the smell of running water.
The whiteness of your beard increases, your hands
are thin, and still you wait.

Translated by Alan Sillitoe

SLOW BUT SURE

Slow but sure the insane light
transforms itself to sanity. So
autumn comes, followed by winter.
Even heretics give thanks
over the radiant balm. The sea has pulled
a long way back. The copper has dimmed. Thunder
lurks in its tunnels.

Slow but sure a painter
paints the white on whitewashed walls. Flecks
of white pepper my beard. The light
is delicate as if after paralysis. Thunder
like an express train will charge out of tunnels:
fear will strike no man, nor dolphin, the honey
dimming like amber too ancient
to be remembered.

Translated by Alan Sillitoe

A FLOOD-TIDE FACES US

A flood-tide faces us. Do not
put us to the test: our ears are seashells, seaweed
and sand between our toes. A flood-
tide faces us, the gull-screams fill
the spaces of our heart. Even if we
wanted to we couldn't hear. A flood-tide
faces us, and the cities spread behind. Do not
put us to the test, transient children like a passing shadow.
Our eyes are golden, a naked flame on
our flesh. The flood-tide
faces us and our cities
spread behind.

Translated by Alan Sillitoe

SMALL BONES ACHE

Small bones ache. A small
pain gnaws, needing no metaphors. A
country small in its love grows towards
hunger.

Nights' candles are no candles
for the night. A map carved in the bones
is not valid when examined. Small
bones ache.

Names are being obscured. Hunger nags. Pain
calls with the voice of a small turtledove. With
fingers of grease and dust
blind people trace countries of light upon
a map of skin.

Candles are extinguished. Small bones
ache.

Translated by Ruth Fainlight

SLOWLY THE EDGES CHANGE

Slowly the edges change to stone. Maybe
the blood is tired of making
its round. Maybe Jerusalem
presses its aging body on Tel
Aviv with longings that fulfil
its ends. Jasmin
will sweeten stony rims, pine
will perfume lattices. Slowly
times and places change, necks
of camels and aircraft. Already the head
looks chiselled. Still the fingers
sing.

Translated by Keith Bosley

WRITING IN A NOTEBOOK

Out from the olives, through the dusty green,
the breeze bears the dates of absolute justice,
before the reckoning and after.
I write in a notebook: After noon, about 2,
I saw a hare skipping towards the wild wheat;
at 2.17 a tortoise;
and a partridge–I didn't note the time–running in terror.
Plenty of observations for a nature-lover;
I am left empty-handed.

And next day there were the military exercises.
The children had serious faces,
they went down as instructed to the shelters, came out as instructed
to cultivated land, sweet air, the price of victory.
I write in a notebook: Before noon, about 8.30,
I saw a child running for cover in the belly of reinforced concrete;
at 8.47 he was free;
and a woman–I didn't note the time–running in terror.
Plenty of qualms for a humanitarian;
I am left, as usual, empty-handed.

Translated by Keith Bosley

TRANSPARENT THROUGH THE WINDOW

Transparent through the window
and bright, the first rain falls.
The earth has heavy hips,
it sinks into her.

Slowly I watch. The fingers
of my right hand open and out of them
a book drops. The first
rain falls. Bright
the window and on the back
of the armchair, so transparent and light
death's hand rests.

Beyond the window the earth
is heavy and her hips ripen.
I shall sink into her.

Translated by Keith Bosley

TONIGHT WE'LL BE BRIGHT AND CLEAR

Tonight we'll be bright and clear on the coastal plain.
At noon the wind still shakes leaden birds, still
the rain with a blind man's grey fingers feels
the face of the earth.

The wind winds us up. Below the face of the earth
bulbs of rare flowers ripen. In spring
they will rise from dead men's eyes. Their names are lost
in the wind and it goes round and round.

Out of a blind man's opened fingers birds
of lead drip on the face of the earth. It is still
noon, foolish heart, be heavy
in my breast as a lump of lead. On the coastal plain
night lingers. Cold and bright, names
of rare flowers rise
from dead men's eyes, maybe
already on the mountains, maybe with the wind.

Translated by Keith Bosley

A MAN WALKS

A man walks behind his dog
as if following after his destiny, enters
a small municipal park as if letting himself
fall into the hands of fate.

The dog comes to a halt. So
does the man. Only the trees
in the park sway
in the light wind.

When the palm opens,
something flies out–someone's
soul perhaps, or a bird.

Translated by Seymour Mayne

OCTOBER 1973

In the vault of heaven this morning
strange birds are flying. Don't hesitate: record
the schedules and objectives. The vault
of heaven is torn by strange cries
this morning. Don't hesitate: record
the sounds and vibrations. This morning
strange trees struggle towards the vault of heaven.
        Don't
hesitate: record the outlines and shades of colour.
        In times to come
neither on sand nor water will it be recorded how
war grips the sky in the thin hands
of pain, how the transparent morning multiplies
despair and hope in their simplicity. Don't hesitate,
        you who obsessively count roots and light years:
in the vault of heaven this morning
strange birds are flying.

Translated by Seymour Mayne

THE LEAVES OF THE OLIVE TREE

The leaves of the olive tree open
like sails in the wind, and often
they are more silver than green
and sometimes greener,
when I look at them I must
disturb their balance,
they are no longer sails then
but become eyes of children
who long to cross green and silver seas
and never can
since their grey eyelashes have been
closed, and they wither in hiding.

Translated by Elaine Feinstein

LIPS ARE RELUCTANT TO SPEAK

Lips are reluctant to speak a single
word of love.
Pain reaches even the fingertips
when thunder clatters, or a bursting shell
fragments the pale horizon.
The aerials of the breeze continually comb
the tangled brush. It is the start of summer,
perhaps the last of spring, a dry
distress carrying neither the code
nor the key to it, in which
the lips are reluctant to speak
even a single word of love.

Translated by Alan Sillitoe

GREEN IDLE WATERS

"Ay, Guadalquivir!"
F.G. Lorca

Green, idle waters,
and in the plaza, Maimonides
sinks down into powerful thoughts,
his face
turned toward Tiberias of sound sleep
where the answers are.

From the East will come, not Magi,
but disgusting lechers to seduce dark women
with an oleander burning on each heart,
to uncover sweet nakednesses
and beget, among arches,
a dark hatred, horrible in metal mantillas
and sharply pointed hoods.

Translated by Denis Johnson

REVOLUTIONS CRACK UP PEOPLE

Revolutions crack up people.
Stones remain closed, calm
in the coolness of their indifference, among orchids
smouldering in the act of identifying with a cause.

From the top of Cabo Girão, under the umbrella
        pines, the sea
seduces to a spectacular finish. People
are cracking up, even breaking. Their strength
is not the strength of stones.

Recomeçar ... let us start from the beginning.

Madeira, Fall 1974

Translated by Seymour Mayne

A PARK

An old Englishman feeds birds
in St. James' Park:
sparrows and pigeons are
nourished in his hand.
His fingers are
almost still, the pale sun
enters the transparent skin,
the rustle of feathers,
like a small sea licking
the edges of
a life.

I also feed birds
in St. James' Park:
I fail:
my fingers are
too shaky and my skin
too foreign, though pale
now in the waters
of this sun;
a paper I read this morning
rustles in my eyes,
my stubborn oriental
wars pursue me.
It's a well known fact
that birds
shy away from nervous
people.

Translated by Anthony Rudolf

LAND'S END, CORNWALL

Land's End.
A step, and already the infinite
blues, greens, greys, gull-shivering, torn by cries.
Perhaps from this rock were seen,
breaking the fog, Israelite ships.
Perhaps on sombre Semitic hair
clung tenuous salts.
Now a chance tourist
emits names of honey and milk,
promises of a lost land
on arid lips.
A step, and the hope of retreat
is the cry of gulls, beyond the reach of language,
deeper than memory. Land's
End, edge. No
further.

Translated by Francis Landy

SQUILLS

The radio announces
squills are in bloom
along the coastal plain,
their shoots thrusting
through the parched soil.

They also say
after death, fingernails
keep growing.

Translated by Barbara Goldberg

KIBBUTZ

And as the evening descended, gentle
almost apologetic rain began to fall
and the scent of mown grass drifted
up from the ground. Afterwards it stopped
and people emerged dressed up
in white shirts—ancient sand
had tempered their flesh
and scratched painful rings in their skin
as if it were the trunk of a tree.
As they walked toward the scent of wet grass
they hailed each other with greetings
of the holiday season.

In the morning the sky was free of blame.
From within the grass the bulbul bird warbled
its song of indifferent triumph and the innocent
light snuggled up to human eyelids
of sandstone, plucked
from the eyes of mica.

Translated by Seymour Mayne

MESSIAH

Along the coastal highway, as in an artery,
electric currents are tearing. Out there
the sea is dark and empty;
and one opens one's palm fearfully:
a nail here on the plain is like a nail on the hill.

Translated by Seymour Mayne

THE PANHANDLE OF GALILEE

"And Joab the son of Zeruiah, and the servants of David, went out, and met together by the pool of Gibeon: and they sat down, the one on the one side of the pool, and the other on the other side of the pool. And Abner said to Joab, Let the young men now arise, and play before us. And Joab said, Let them arise."

Second Samuel, 2:13,14

The Dan River loosens, cool between
raspberry bushes, and does not reach
hot Beersheba.
On its banks boys tangle with
girls, casting Samuel II and those longings
into an elderly poet's lap.

In vain he tries to snare them
with baited words. Bronzed and sure
they push past him and under smooth skin
their muscles jigger like lightning.

In a rage of love he shapes them
for safekeeping. The Dan pours between
raspberry bushes, and they are taken
unaware. Stiff-fingered
the poet caresses the
page and in their hot blood
a sudden shiver moves.

Translated by Anat Feinberg

ISRAELI LOVE POEM

From one war to the next
my beloved's face is dissolving. Already
it is impossible for me to congeal the colour of her eyes,
the shadow of her hair. It seems to me that only
the evening is as blue as it used to be.

Downstairs once again they are being called up
according to their height, not according to the bite
of their mouths. How many floors are now freezing
between us, the observer from the balcony and the other
preparing to execute the order down on the street? The ranks
get into line. Soon
military boots will thud in uniform
rhythm. It seems to me that the evening
is as blue as it used to be. You were loved,
it seems to me.

Translated by Seymour Mayne

EXHIBITION POSTER

I noticed a poster of an exhibition by Ludwig
Blum. Not Joyce's or Dublin's Bloom. Jerusalem's
and Blum's Blum. Two green cypresses and the violet depth
of firm hills. An old poster, from even
before the last war.

And I was thinking that I would like to stop
between the two cypresses as at a station, and fill up
with green breath and gently penetrate with force
the depth of these firm hills, and then gratified
        grow slowly violet
so that the next war will tarry. I was thinking that
        the war will tarry
and perhaps pass overhead like the shadow
of a cloud or the palm of a hand that has
and has not touched. From the depths, Blum,
I called out to you.

Translated by Seymour Mayne

SHALOM*

Two syllables shorter than the grass
in a world noisy with big words. Transparent
light courses through their arteries without benefit
of angels striking them on their humble heads, without
a genealogical tree offering shelter in its shade.

Beloved, white is already creeping into your hair
like frost from a distant land
while the palms of your warm hands
open and the grass rustles. Up front there
tall soldiers pass.

A wind has come to rest upon your heart
and then departed. Only these two
syllables still nestle there,
shorter than the grass, lighter
than the light.

March 26, 1979
(The day the peace agreement
was signed between Israel and Egypt.)

Translated by Seymour Mayne

**Peace*, in Hebrew

III

1980-1986

ALCHEMISTS

Stones do not transmute into gold.
Not because they lack desire
or strength, but because alchemists,
hunters of the sun, reckoners of the Era
of Wonders, trace veins of red marble
in a half-hearted fashion. Sand trickles
uselessly from their scorched fingers. Stones
do not transmute into gold because seekers
of secrets stand baffled as children
before half-charted maps. Those in charge
of hope are hopeless, and even unicorns
sprout two horns from the forehead
for the sake of balance. Stones do not
transmute into gold, the wand is flawed,
the salamander recoils from fire, lust
sparked by mandrake roots twists back
into itself, the eyes in the skull
are vacant, and the distant sea keens
a lament all night, not even one
purple sail on the paling horizon.

Translated by Barbara Goldberg

AFTER THE HOLIDAYS

After the holidays, she said, after
the hills, the plain, the sea, after
clouds bearing the scent of rain
like tidings, after wet grass, not wet
anymore, after the holidays, he said,
after the eyes, starred flesh, the ice
climbing despite the climate into
the bones, after the maps, marvelously
detailed with memories of death, after
the holidays, she said. The holidays came
and went, indifferent tenants who don't
look back, while in a vase on her vanity
compulsory promises fade. After the holidays
he said, after the holidays, she said.

Translated by Barbara Goldberg

TOWARD EVENING

Toward evening a vacant man looks out
into the world. He sees nothing, no gold,
no fire. Perhaps he remembers a brightness,
but only dimly, and through a haze. Then
he turns on his way, vacant as before.
His foot won't stumble on gold, therefore
he won't fill his pockets. Fire won't scorch
his face because he keeps it well-hidden
from the elements. His eyes won't brim
with tears. Vacant, he returns to a house
where darkness waits at the threshold
to envelop him, to take him in.

Translated by Barbara Goldberg

JONAH

Tonight the sea will become heavy, I know, and on
its surface fogs will sail like phantom
ships in which ancient moons will faintly
shine. I shall count the ships one by one
without even moving my lips. Thus Jonah
stood on the coast of Joppa, freezing and mutely
counting
the Hebrew times of his refusal. And then
a boat swallowed him in the fog and in due course
towards clear spaces that were not his
the whale expelled a dim amber moon and the message
and the curse. Tonight the sea will become heavy,
I know.

Translated by Seymour Mayne

INEVITABILITY

Dreadful is the inevitability of time. Look
at the palms of your hands, the backs of your
        hands, see how
sunspots are sprinkled over your body's
        flameless landscape.
Tel Aviv is sand, is salt, is a passing dream,
is the picture of a moon that froze in darkness.
And you? You are the bay of a forehead that
        expanded inward
where tired thoughts yearn to cast anchor
in the face of possible storms. Dreadful is
time in its inevitability.

Translated by Edna Sharoni

BORDER

On this northern border the passports of our
lives
have expired. Only the wrinkles that circle
your eyes
are extended to the wrinkles that crosscut my
heart. My
impossible one, when the merciless ice
freezes all channels of contact how
shall I grope towards you, and you towards
me? Not
even one belated word of love shall I know
how to speak to you in your tongue, nor how
to thaw out in stealth one rivulet of
blood, to arouse one single flower of
deceptive spring to rebel against the lawful,
suitable frost.
The wrinkles that circle my eyes are extended
to the wrinkles that crosscut your heart. Only
the passports of our lives have expired on this
border,
in the north.

Translated by Edna Sharoni

A ROMAN FRESCO

And when, with voices
of wild birds, the crowd
cries *He is at the gates!*
Alas! He is at the gates!
how do Senators in purple-
hemmed togas react?
How pale the Consul's face
grows! Doesn't the heart
of the bravest Centurion feel
as if clenched in a fist?

But the air keeps on
going blue like a vein
in the thigh of the most
beloved of Gallic slaves
and along the well-kept banks
the poplars are silvery.
Only the gaze of the Dictator,
turning inward toward his own
time and the possibilities
hidden in it, darkens
like the waters of a river
when a chilly night
alights upon it.

Translated by Mark Whitcis Holm

MARCUS AURELIUS (121-180)

Marcus Aurelius Antoninus, when about to
depart
from the world, meditates: I the Stoic have
wearied
of aggression and violence, and I, Caesar,
have warred
against the Parthians, Sarmatians, the Quadi
and Marcomanni
and defended the borders of the Empire. My
wife Faustina
whom I loved and who bore me eleven
children
betrayed me in secret. Faithful to my
philosophy
I took care to hate no man and my palace
became a den
of slander and fraud. Nor do I know of what
I am dying, of the stomach disease that has
racked me
for many days, or of the poison concocted by
command of my son
Commodus. My *Meditations,* which I wrote at
every
free moment, in the frenzy of governing, at
the outbreak
of battles that swayed the fate of the Empire,
are apt
to immortalize me more than the Antonine
Column, and all
hastens to pass–fame and glory together.
Behold
I am dying and my tyrant son, who loves
gladiators like
his very soul, will rule in my place. Indeed
death is rest
from the strife of the senses, from cares which
fray the nerves,
from the labour of constant thought, from
thralldom to needs of the flesh.

Translated by Edna Sharoni

FROM THE OUTSET

And from the outset it was clear that there is
no
purpose. A particle of heat shimmered to the
heights
as though climbing toward goals that cannot
be reached.
The verdict is not likely to be changed, it
cannot
be: the Persian lilac thicket is bare, and will
remain so.
And this was clear from the beginning.
When it was said that the end of this city
is extinction there was no longer any doubt
that this refers both to you and to me, to this
body
aging towards the finish line,
to the palpable tree from childhood, to the
slivers
of heat diffused all about, to the taste
of personal blood of the sacrificed for whom a
substitute
is provided only in the ancient Sources.

Translated by Edna Sharoni

TRACK

The railroad track goes wherever it goes
all the seasons of the year: in their white
helmets the sentry-blossoms of the squills are
        an escort
lovely and useless to those who accept the
        fate
of railroad ties and tracks.

At home this evening we shut the windows
that face to north and west: the sea appeared
        to be plotting
dark schemes and we have known for long that
out of the north shall the evil break forth.

November 1981

Translated by Edna Sharoni

OLIVE TREES

Olive trees walk like a band of black-clad
monks,
tormentedly bearing their tapers of incense,
they walk twisted, disjointed, crumbling
to their bitter, wintry exile
beyond hills and wadis and canyons,
spied by jackals with yellowing coppery eyes,
olive trees walk black like men
and their silence is darkness.

Translated by Edna Sharoni

LETTERS

When the earth was still covered with water,
someone drew his name there, as a child would,
in block letters. Long afterward, when the earth
dried off, the letters were inscribed as if in rock,
as if from the age of an ancient king. Later,
there came the ones who overpowered the earth
with their shoes, and after them dogs with their claws,
and the wild grasses. And then the falling leaves served
as a mantle, tenderly cast down over the faces
of the dead while the good earth caused the bones
of the dead ones to feel at ease. And a long,
a fruitful sleep fell upon them. He who looks now
will see only the bare rudiments of a name,
he will remember that something heroic happened here.
And these will be sufficient for him because he
is only a traveler or because these are signs enough
for the wandering poet.

Translated by Myra Sklarew

RESPONSIBILITY

At my feet a female dog lies as if in an old English
painting. Through my window, for the first time
in many days, transparent air flows in. You know,
perhaps we misread our time, this place. Perhaps
we were meant to breathe in a different rhythm, to use
different words. Now the wind passes without
any resistance in a sky emptied of planes and no one
shouts to us "Halt!" And no one wonders
how it is possible to pass in this way, without even one
shout of warning or the rattle of a rifle lock or the thud
of soldiers' boots, heavy with responsibility,
as they approach the barricades.

Translated by Myra Sklarew

TWO POEMS FROM A DISTANT LAND

I

FOXES

When northern oaks and maples
barter their green for blood and gold,
what are northern foxes up to?
At night they slip in to little Michel
and lick his cheek with their warm tongues.

Grey and black and silver
foxes from the far north:
steal in silently, loyal friends,
and nuzzle against the palms of his dream.

Translated by Seymour Mayne

II

SWAN

The water still flows in the Rideau. With widespread
fingers of water the river catches flaming
torches of leaves and puts them out with a kiss.
Citizens, do not worry: no
conflagration will break out here.

And out in the current, floating motionless,
a swan turns white as if out of Mallarmé:
prisoner of its own will before the freeze sets in,
the stately creature ignores the warning cries
of a rabble of sea-gulls.

Only the stranger, passing on his way, hears
mountains closing in on the town;
in the depths of the forests rustle
the primeval breath of ambushers.

Translated by Seymour Mayne

LET US REMEMBER THE NAMES

Let us remember the names: Neil
Armstrong and Edwin E. Aldrin. They
were the first humans who placed their feet
on the moon. In the photo of July 21st 1969 we can see
the prints of their soles on the ground. Afterwards, after
meticulous tests, it was proved beyond doubt
that the moon is an absolutely dead star.

What good therefore to poetize over
a precious crescent walking, Selene sister
of the sun god, Artemis the virgin huntress
chaste of kisses?
Fear, deep in the crevices of our brains, alone
nourishes the beliefs in the lunar causation of
epilepsy and madness. Indeed, when the moon
is full, if we gaze very hard, we can sometimes notice
a kind of human visage stamped like a brand of Cain on the mask
of its cold dispassionate face.

Translated by Richard Flantz

WHEN POETS DIE

"Mathematics is written only for mathematicians."
Nicholas Copernicus (1473-1543)

When poets die lines do not change.
Latitude does not expand, longitude remains
as it was. The earth circles
the sun.

When poets die tin and gold do not change
their substance. Light and darkness
assimilate as before death.
The first rain knocks
on the windowpane and the short autumn
will soon be gathered to the winds of the sea.

When poets die what lines
shackle them to the land of tin and gold?
In first rain they dissolve like webs
of light and darkness. If the earth circles
the sun, the astronomer is he who said:
there will be change.
Mathematics is written only
for mathematicians. For whom
poetry?

Translated by Anat Feinberg

LEADERSHIP

What is so smart in following a strong leader?
He is strong and we are weak. He gives orders
and we submit. It is better to follow
weak leaders. We take pity and they are pitiful.
How warm we feel when compassionate and leaning
on each other we sense how strength grows
within us. When we stand like this,
all together, the horizon moves closer.

Translated by Seymour Mayne

DUSK, JUNE 1982

Violet is the dusk over Tel Aviv like iodine
spilling over the horizon pierced by hotel towers.
Violet is the absurd head of the hydra, Mediterranean
and persistent in its growth. Violet are the helicopters
bursting out of a womb of water and metal.
Violet are the sounds of the jukebox
announcing to the street seven kinds
of ice-cream and death.

Translated by Seymour Mayne

I AM A BIRD

"I am a bird who was once a poet."
Roger Zelazny, *The Lord of Light*

I am a bird who was once a poet.
You probably won't notice it, but to
the tips of my birdhood I can sense how
the poet I once was flaps about
in my heart. When the sun touches my feathers
I begin saying poetry, without willing to
I sing and sing to the light
that blinds. You probably won't notice it,
but when the cool mercies of night enwrap the
burning of my eyes, I, the bird who was once
a poet, sense in dread how a new
song already starts climbing like a thief in my
finely plumed breast, setting the cords
of my charred throat aquiver so as to
flame up again at dawn. Does a poet
who once was a bird beat so with his arms,
try so, without respite, to raise himself
above this heavy earth?

Translated by Richard Flantz

IV

New Poems

BASIC COLOUR

A wintry morning glowing like the inside
of a pearl. The small globe of white light
is self-contained like a photograph
of Tel Aviv, the little one, refusing to expand.

At night the storm howled with the voices
of horrible, mythic birds.
Now the sea is quiet, as if nothing has happened,
wrapping itself in aesthetic greens and blues: the red
danger rag waving above the lifeguard's
empty shack simply adds a basic colour, not a warning
of things to come or a foolish reassurance.

And a breeze is wiping out the footsteps on the beach
        and there is no
Robinson to feel his heart suddenly stop
when he sees them, in light like the light of a pearl
bleeding over the rim.

Translated by Jean Nordhaus

SOIL

"John Synge, I and Augusta Gregory thought
All that we did, all that we said or sang
Must come from contact with the soil, from that
Contact everything Antaeus-like grew strong."

William Butler Yeats
"The Municipal Gallery Revisited"

I passed there a decade ago.
Under thin, incessant rains,
the arthritis of poor streets keeps flaring up
and in horizon-strangling Catholic fog
the land of Cuchulain
withdraws to the isles of the west.
From what soil now
will the heirs of the mystic rose draw strength,
poet, diviner, disdainer of rabble?

A decade has passed. How important is this grain
of time? There, as here, the sanctifying
fog rolls in from all sides, enfolding
the poets as well as the masses.
And what can stop it when it starts to spread,
what wall hold back the sea-monsters, its children,
if the heel no longer knows that touch of power:
sand, clay-red and yellow loam, black clods heavy with promise,
earth strewn with stones like dragon-teeth?

Without the soil we grow abstract and fade: mould
of the body, rose from whose roots a sun of gold breaks forth,
snake-killer, dispeller of mists.

Translated by Jean Nordhaus

FACES

Down
in the sand
you bite my foot.
And if your foot
were on my face?
We are bound
by ropes of venom,
the chambers
of our hearts filling
with clots of dark
thoughts.
Perhaps our children
will know better
encounters than this
between sand and sea,
under great stars.
For now,
let there be
silence
between us
on the face
of this
bitter
sand.

Translated by Mark Whiteis Helm

GIANTS

Behold them, giants with feet of clay, arbiters
of destiny, seated around a table where, above
their resting arms, their faces are secure
in calm, as through the open French window flow
the scent of lilac and the passing of the hours.

See how huge they are, there in the open summer,
how vast the distance between their tranquil brows
in which the arteries of thought
pulse with an enviable regularity,
and the feet of clay,
almost invisible in the shadow of the table.

Translated by Henry Taylor

RECRUITS

Once I stood at attention among green recruits and heard the
sergeant say,
"If any man here can translate from English, let him take one
step forward."
I stepped forward. And was sent to clean sewers with my bare
hands.
"The job suits intellectuals," the sergeant said, and laughed until
he choked
when I dipped my hands in the gutter.

In the long years since, I have translated English poetry,
fiction, even
essays on the Art of War, and still, I stand at attention,
an eternal recruit, a draftee forever. And when Sarge
asks his question, I still step forward smartly,
even though I know by now I will be sent again to clean
a gutter with my bare hands.

Conditioned reflex? Or a shining example to patriots?
Either way, the job suits intellectuals:
that choking laughter isn't the sergeant's any more.
It's mine.

Translated by Henry Taylor

EXCAVATIONS

The sky has turned into an iron dome.
Fierce gales drive from west to east, harbingers
of beautiful murderous Europe. Anxiously
we searched the armoured horizon for banners
of the new crusaders. Then we resumed
our dig in the hard soil for shards
of history, coins for testimony, sarcophagi
whose bones we prize, confirming
covenants, for the sake of the future.

Translated by Barbara Goldberg

HISTORY

You talk to me about History: tombs
of kings take on dusk's saffron robes,
and the hard flesh of the land peels off
bones of rock, erodes to the sea.

You keep on talking about History: haze presses down
on us like an oxygen mask and already I can't tell
whether these are ripened oranges rolling on the ground
or shrunken, decapitated, amber heads.

Translated by Barbara Goldberg

THE EMPEROR

Fires were seen beyond the frontier. The border stones
remain undisturbed. The land is peaceful. Up high
in the watchtowers, sentries scan the horizon,
detecting hints of fire more than fire,
the possibility of conflagration.

Nevertheless, the news is dutifully reported
to the ministers, and they, in phrases fit
for exalted ears, phrases at once official
and imprecise, inform the Emperor. His heavy lids
veil his eyes as he listens, reclining
on dark velvet cushions fringed with gold.

Like night butterflies, faint strains of lutes
flutter, perhaps from the women's wing.

If there were fires, they burned from an inconceivable
distance. Possibly a few nomads, wrapped
in foul furs, bowlegged from long days
in the saddle, huddled around them,
grunting in a coarse primitive tongue.
The border stones are in place.
The land is peaceful.

Now, after the ministers have departed, humbly
bowing again and again, the Emperor opens his eyes.
Lute tones fall and fade away. Perhaps all this
is a mere flicker of light and shadow
in a large, half-darkened room, kindling
the dilated pupils with memories of fire,
too remote to be apprehended.

Translated by Barbara Goldberg

ABISHAG

"Let there be sought for my lord the king a
young virgin...that my lord the king may get heat."
First Kings, 1:2

When David is cold, Abishag
lies in his bosom.
And when Abishag is cold?

With the patience of small stones
and roots of love-grass, the earth
will embrace David and Abishag
until they grow warm.

Translated by Barbara Goldberg

LOCAL FLORA

The Israeli Oak
is Israeli. The Gilboa Iris
grows exclusively on Mount Gilboa:
not just any tree or any flower,
but distinctively native. Indeed
the Israeli Oak *(Pistacia Palaestina)*
and the Gilboa Iris *(Irus Hayeni)*
are from a world view, nearly
unknown, and as to the specificity
of their locale, that has borne
dire consequences: on the Gilboa
that day most likely extravagant
with irises, King Saul fell
onto his sword, suffering mightily
until the young Amalekite slew him,
and while riding under the boughs
of a great oak, Absalom and his
abundant hair became entangled
in a terrible trap of love
from which there was no letting go.

Translated by Barbara Goldberg

THE COMMANDER

All night heavy vehicles kept rolling on–
tanks, artillery, ammunition and
equipment trucks, fuel tankers.
The offensive is set to begin
just after first light. The Commander-in-Chief
has held the casualty estimates in his hand
and pondered them, tight-lipped.
He foresees the outcome, and still
his orders stand. Has he ever read
For Whom the Bell Tolls? We will
never know. What we know is that heavy
vehicles rolled all night, and at sunrise, when
the troops began to move out, the purity
of light dawning in the Commander's window
drew him to the curtain to look,
and he clapped a hand over his eyes as if
he had stared into the heart of fire.

Translated by Henry Taylor

LIZARD

Like a lizard alternately
stretching his neck out and pulling it in,
I keep craning for prospects
of rain or clearing skies.
Sun, take pity on us civilized reptiles;
do not deny us, too, your warmth and light.

Translated by Jean Nordhaus

ROBINSON JEFFERS (1887-1962)

Robinson Jeffers, American, at Carmel,
California, built a tower from sea
stones on top of cliffs overlooking
the ocean and there, isolated
from commotion, settled
down and wrote his poems.

But even there, on the wild
beautiful beach, he was surrounded:
first, by an artists' colony,
later, by the industry of war.

Translated by Mark Whiteis-Helm

OVER IOWA CITY

On the opalescent sky
over Iowa City, over gardens
of flaming gold, a child
or a poet had scrawled:
Writers of the World, Unite!

This was considered inflammatory;
for municipal firefighters
were put on full alert
and worked long hours overtime
to douse these words,
so revolutionary, so intimate.

Translated by Barbara Goldberg

HANG GLIDER

In the Shenandoah sky
a hang glider pilot looks
down, sees a Persian rug
of fire, colours changing
with the modulation of wind.
Quickly, he makes letters
from clouds and hangs out
an azure sheet announcing
an unprecedented end of season
sale on Oriental carpets.

Translated by Mark Whiteis-Helm

COLOURS

"All American dollar bills are green."
Information for tourists, U.S. Government publication

See how America turns crimson, gold, violet,
drapes herself like ancient royalty
in arrogant purple, denies her own
forebears and the revered
principles of the Constitution.

Only the dollar stays green, impervious
to the changing seasons, migrations
of birds and people and the merciless
erosion of sea rocks and skyscrapers.

Translated by Barbara Goldberg

SEA SLUGS

Research on sea slugs found
nothing more powerful than the urge
to repeat. If true for us, our lives
would be less intricate, simpler, closer
to the elements, rich with smells
of iodine, salt, seaweed and shells.
What disrupts the serenity of slugs,
arouses a yearning for something
abstract like horizons, sunsets
of a different palette, lures us
out of sluggishness, moves us to risk
what we call progress? Scientists
say a force that overcomes
habit is love.

Oh my sea slug, moist and salty,
now that science has proclaimed
its verdict, shall we
kiss and start crawling?

Translated by Barbara Goldberg

NEW BABYLON

Scientists of climate believe
the world's temperature is gradually
climbing, polar caps are melting
and the frozen arctics are
steadily shrinking. We have proof!
bright pure skies as before original sin,
                                        and in the supermarket
glow apples, pears, raspberries, strawberries
under the steady gleam of a paradise
that never heard of flaming swords.

Why then, are you so woeful, brief Sojourner, why
over and over do you look toward the North with
                                        frightened eyes? What
map of anxiety traced in God-forsaken places
thousands of years ago by bearded medicine men
wrapped in flaking animal skins
now traps your steps
on the sidewalks of New Babylon?

Translated by Ann Darr

YOU SAY BIG WORDS

You say big words: world, race,
history. I think small: breast,
thigh, pudenda.

You move from left to right and I
from right to left. Therefore
there's a chance we'll meet, either
at some historic crossroad, or
on the nearest couch.

Translated by Barbara Goldberg

FIRST DRAFT

The first draft of the body
is read in hotels where secret
agents pose as receptionists,
in cars parked on backroads
swept by a non-biblical flood
of leaves, in office buildings
crumbling under their own anonymity,
under neon moons. And we do not hope
anymore for anything, and already
we have discarded previous drafts,
ensuing chapters, interpretations
clarifying intent, the illuminating
footnote. We grope for each other
like two blind moles, our tangled
tongues murmuring rudimentary sounds
of a beginning alphabet, syllables
of flesh, syllables of blood.

Translated by Barbara Goldberg

MAPS

The map of the motherland is engraved
on bones, retina, sunspots, on the skin's
scroll. But that other geography, soft
hillocks whose tips stiffen at the first
sign of storm, fertile valleys, their sweet
waters, dark woods? The map to that country
has not yet been charted. We wrap ourselves
up in it like two frightened children,
our stammering fingers tracing the wrinkles,
the winding routes, and with mouths filled
as if with burning coals, our slow tongues
learn to articulate the inviolate places.

Translated by Barbara Goldberg

SALE

At the mall everything is sold: electric
appliances, clothes, furniture, jewelry, toys,
food for human and animal consumption, antique
despair, renewed hope. Only the following
items cannot be found: that pearl-grey
colour of the sky, the way your claws
retract when first your nimble fingers
trip up my spine, then down the front.

Translated by Barbara Goldberg

DIVERS

With commingled limbs, skin
still moist and bearing
the smell of each other,
we surface out of the depths
of love and emerge, blinking
into light. The rim of the world
is sprinkled with a fine powder
of frost, and the faithful dog
barks at our entry, as though
we were strangers. We must learn
all over again to navigate
on land, to speak an everyday
language, to breathe like those
who cannot dive, like two
landlocked creatures, even
before the breach of winter.

Translated by Barbara Goldberg

ENDANGERED SPECIES

My forefathers reckoned the End
of Days. I content myself with more
humble calculations, those brief
and terrified moments which flock
to your riverbed and crevices
like endangered species seeking
refuge, until I come to gather
them into the fold, an impassioned
shepherd with a pitiless love.

Translated by Barbara Goldberg

THE LAST INCH

Do you really crave to learn
the last inch of my body? Please
don't. Curb your excessive appetite
for knowledge. Leave something
to placate the jealous gods, a morsel
of skin, a few fibers of flesh, a drop
of blood. Better still, don't study
at all. A worn body, what beauty
or wisdom can it possess? Accept it
as a token gift, and don't ask
where it came from, or for whom
it was intended. Listen instead
to the wild heartbeat, the trembling
fingers, and be content. Pull away
your hand and go. If you seem to hear
a stifled sob, a sigh of someone
in pain, don't look back. It's only
the wind trapped in bare branches,
first struggling, then tearing itself
loose, as though nothing has happened.

Translated by Barbara Goldberg

SIEGE

Even without the unexpected snowfall
we would feel like a town under siege,
defending itself from marauding tribes
descending from steppes, the uncertain horizon.
Now prisoners of a refined architecture,
the columnar austerity of snow,
we are more conscious than ever
of our clumsiness, our faulty manners.
You therefore have to forgive me
if my face flushed when you entered,
and I failed by gesturing too bluntly
or speaking too harshly. I expect
it is the result of the prolonged
siege, not a sudden dimming of the senses,
rather the flowering of a middle-aged fool
in the heart of a wintry landscape.

Translated by Barbara Goldberg

TATTOO

After long arduous hours, the old
tattoo craftsman Chen Ying Chen
completes his design: an iridescent
dancer opens and shuts her fan
as the biceps flex or extend.

My little Chinese, how swiftly
your intricate topography was tattooed
on my skin. Now those fierce hills
and harmonious valleys keep pace
with my muscles, and the sweet
cave with its buried strongbox
waits in darkness for the opening.

Translated by Barbara Goldberg

GLASS DREAM

When touched by light, your glass dream
chimes with the sound of tiny bells
and your nipples, like two dark Chinese
copper butterflies, flutter, first one
then the other. The Mandarin's city
slumbers in the distance, its soldiers
and tax collectors still prisoners
of sleep. A breeze drifts in
from the river. The curtains swell
with lilac. We are sailing.

Translated by Barbara Goldberg

COALMAN

Lady, if I were your coalman,
on raw wintry mornings I would stop
at your door, as in old stories,
and fill up your entire cellar
with my coals, in order to keep you
warm; and cap in hand, I would pour
a few extra hard black lumps
into your palm, the one that fits
so snugly in your fur glove. You,
lady, would first be confused, then
astounded at the sudden radiance
glowing between your fingers.
The severe intensity of my love
has done that. It is well known
that enormous pressure transforms
coal into diamonds, in a prolonged
inevitable way, far removed from human
sight, deep in the earth's throat.

Translated by Barbara Goldberg

NO, PLEASE DON'T

No, please don't die over me
or for me. Go on being
what you are, sweetcunt, easy
charmer, the same miraculous
flint, *shamir*, that sundered
King Solomon's stones. Please
don't die, don't. It's enough
that each day I die my little deaths.
You, please, as best you can, keep
your stunning mix of toughness
and fragility, that stiffens
and melts my loins, my soul, whenever
I'm struck by the electric thought
of you, sweetcunt, easy charmer,
shamir, my life, my death, my love.

Translated by Barbara Goldberg

HARD WATER

We have harder water, harder
soil, harder stars, we have
harder women.

You seduce us
with softer water, softer
stars, you seduce us
with softer women.

When Jacob wrestled the angel, his soles
pummeled hard soil, hard water seeped
into ditches, hard stars tumbled down,
entangling themselves in the hard hair
of his beard. He was nearly vanquished
when the angel, weary, and with faltering breath
described Rachel's soft breasts, the sweet
slopes of her belly. Then the stones
that pillowed Jacob's head his solitary
nights of preparation before Canaan, gathered
together, hardening his bones for the last
crucial effort. No angelic touch bruised
the hollow of his thigh, no one barred
his entry now into the hard promised land.

Translated by Barbara Goldberg

AT THE WELL

My parched tongue uncovers
the route to your love, moist
and hidden by a cluster
of forget-me-nots.

I shall remember: the sun,
the thirst, the well
from whose mouth
I did not roll off stones.

Translated by Barbara Goldberg

YOUR DIGITAL CLOCK

In your digital clock, minute
after minute drops down the chute
of time, vanishes. I am wrapped
in dark anxiety, disguising itself
as lust. I clutch you and thus
entwined, footsteps that stalk me,
my separate entity, recede. You
with endless compassion gather me
to your lap, your limbs a shield
against names, faces, the creeping
ivy that roots out my existence.
Even you cannot mute my thudding
heart, or blind the owl, his gaze
copper-yellow, incorruptible.

Translated by Barbara Goldberg

TOYS

It's time. Now we shall put on
our smiles, you on your porcelain
princess face, and I on my toy
soldier face.

The city is falling. The wooden houses
in flames, the stone houses, razed.
Down streets littered with corpses
gallop the small horses of the barbarians,
their manes blowing, their teeth bared.

The palace windows are shuttered against
the tumult and stink. The ball commences.
The Grand Duke signals the orchestra
to strike up the royal waltz. It's time
and the two of us, you with your porcelain
princess smile and I with my toy soldier
smile, take the first steps.

Translated by Barbara Goldberg

ARK

From out of the ark on Baba's sheet
the animals march in cheerful pairs,
departing Ararat as on organized tour:
he-elephant, she-elephant; he-rhino,
she-rhino; he-flamingo, she-flamingo.
On Baba's sheet the waters have now
receded, no need to send forth doves
for omens of green. Already the flood
is consigned to memory, as is God's fury
for impious greed. But when I lick salt
off Baba's shoulder, which rests precisely
on Ararat's tip, it seems I hear a faint
echo of hammers and smell fresh shavings
as though the story is bound to repeat
and from the beginning.

Translated by Barbara Goldberg

NAMES

When and how would the High Priest enunciate
the Explicit Name? On the Day of Atonement
after the people, clothed in white, departed
the temple to congregate in the courtyard,
he'd cover his head with the *parochet,**
place it deep inside the niche, then utter
those beloved and sacred syllables, floating
them like tiny vessels into the ark.

At the dawn of the world we, more humble
priests of sun and dunes, dared call out
those three ancient Hebrew syllables, an act
of supreme courage. No lightning bolt
shattered the clear summer sky.

Time flows, green as wormwood. Baba, I
whisper your starry name, its two childish
syllables like a hyphen joining what was
to what will be. Silence. Only a passing
plane disrupts this foreign sky covering
depots, supermarkets, parks and warehouses
like a secular *parochet.*

Your flesh is still warm. If lightning
struck now, surely it would herald
nothing but merciful spring rain.

Translated by Barbara Goldberg

**Parochet,* curtain hung on the ark.

ALTERNATE POSSIBILITIES

Here is the station of alternate
possibilities–one can get off, or
keep on traveling. But a Motherland,
is that subject to choice? A man
carries his passport in his breast
pocket because he craves foreign air,
a sky as singular as the ceiling
of a room he has never slept in,
and in his belly he nurtures
exotic birds, possessions
too precious ever to pawn.

It's impossible, a man says
to himself, to be torn in half,
and unhealthy too. Well, he gets off
or he travels on, and suddenly
instead of familiar road, a lake
imposes itself on his vision.
Cattails brush his lips. He runs
and shouts because his heart
is bursting. The entire earth
encompasses him, and all
his blood is contained within.

The poet is condemned to double
vision, but sand and stone are
sand and stone and have been
since the beginning. They lack
the capacity to forgive. The poet
looks at the man begging for mercy,
begging to be made whole, and tries
to crawl to his brother. He sings
his lament, all the colours
of the world in his mouth.

Translated by Barbara Goldberg

CROSSING THE RIVER

Today we cross the river. Even those
who walk on foot won't find it difficult.
Summer. The waters have greatly receded
and each cattail poking out of the mud
is also mirrored in the shimmering haze.
First march the priests, prophets, soothsayers,
the presidents of the tribes. Then
family leaders, their kin, the slaves,
the sheep and cattle. This is the river,
dark and green. Guide books call it
Yarden, El-Urdan, le jourdain, Jordan,
and it is written it serves as the gate
to the promised land. Surely the books
are right. This morning, moving slowly
from east to west, we saw nomads track us
on the opposite bank, galloping back
and forth, brandishing thin lances made of reed.
Immediately the priests held high the Tablets
of Covenant. The nomads vanished. Perhaps
they were only a mirage. Then we were given
the signal to cross the holy waters.

Translated by Barbara Goldberg

NOTE ON THE AUTHOR

Moshe Dor was born in 1932 in Tel Aviv where he was raised and educated. As a young man he joined the Haganah and served as correspondent for the Israel Army Weekly magazine *Bamahaneh*. Later he studied at the Hebrew University of Jerusalem and the University of Tel Aviv where he completed undergraduate work in Political Science and History.

He was one of the founding members and editors of the *Likrat* ("Toward") group which, comprised of the most important young writers of the early 1950s, promulgated the "New Manner" in Israeli writing. He has published some twenty-five books including volumes of poetry, collections of children's verse, literary essays, and two books of interviews with foreign and Israeli writers. As well, he has translated several works by English, American and Canadian writers. An initial volume of selected poems in English translation, *Maps of Time*, was published in England in 1978.

Moshe Dor has worked as a journalist and for many years was on the editorial board of *Maariv*, one of Israel's leading newspapers. He represented Israel in 1970-71 at the International Writing Program of the University of Iowa, and he has served on the presidium of the Hebrew Writers Association, Israel's Press Council, and the P.E.N. Club, to whose presidency he was elected in 1988. From 1975-77 he was Counsellor for Cultural Affairs at the Embassy of Israel in London, England, and during the fall of 1987 he joined the American University, Washington, D.C., as Distinguished Writer-in-Residence. In 1986 he received the Prime Minister's Award for Creative Writing, and in 1987 the Bialik Prize for *On Top of the Cliff: Selected Poems 1954-86*.

Crossing the River draws on the full range of Moshe Dor's body of work and includes poems written from the 1950s to the present.

BIBLIOGRAPHY: BOOKS BY MOSHE DOR

In Hebrew

Poetry

White Cypresses, 1954
If We Do and If We Don't, 1957
Writ of Attachment, 1960
Street Crossing, 1962
Gold and Ashes, 1963
Nettle and Metal, 1965
Icarus the World, 1966
Baron Porcelli in Jerusalem, 1968
Selected Poems, 1970
Maps of Time, 1975
Kites on Hampstead Heath, 1980
From the Outset, 1984
On Top of the Cliff: Selected Poems 1954-86, 1986
Crossing the River, 1989

Poetry for Children

A Boat of Chocolate Slabs, 1968
Amir's Palace, 1970
Who Would Like to Be a Wizard?, 1975
Day After Day, 1986
The Owl's Party, 1987

Literary Essays

Reading and Re-Reading, 1970

Interviews

Let Other People Know, 1974
Poets Do Not Run in Packs, 1985

Anthology

Same Faces: Contemporary Anglo-Jewish Poets, 1981
(editor and translator)

In English

Poetry

Maps of Time, 1978

Anthology

The Burning Bush: Poems from Modern Israel, 1977
(co-editor)

ACKNOWLEDGEMENTS

Many of these translations first appeared in literary magazines, including *Ariel, Delos, Folio, The Jewish Quarterly, London Magazine, Modern Hebrew Literature, Poet Lore, Stand, The Tel Aviv Review, Tikkun, Webster Review, The World and I,* and in the following anthologies, *Voices Within the Ark* and *Writing from the World.*

The following translations, whose copyright is held by The Menard Press on behalf of the translators, were originally published in *Maps of Time*, The Menard Press, London, 1978: "The Leaves of the Olive Tree", "Lips Are Reluctant to Speak", "The World Shrinks", "Slow but Sure", "A Flood-Tide Faces Us", "Small Bones Ache", "You Are Right, You Know", "Writing in a Notebook", "Slowly the Edges Change", "Transparent through the Window", "Tonight We'll Be Bright and Clear", "A Park", "Land's End, Cornwall", "The Dwelling", "Going Back", "A Demented Tree", "Does David Still Play before You", "Wounds", "Notes for an Armenian Biography", "Morning", and "Green Idle Waters".

The author and editor are grateful to The Menard Press for granting permission to include the above.